Unlck Your
Greatness
— Ms. Meka —

Greatness Now

ISBN: 978-0692933855

ISBN: 0692933859

Special Thanks:

Courtney Artiste, Editor
Purposed Publishing
purposedlife.net

For more information, please visit
www.askmeka.com
or
www.vamekerbanks.com

Contents

7 Keys to Unlock Your Greatness:

Key #1: Have A Dream

Key #2: Think Great Thoughts

Key #3: Elevate Your Effort

Key #4: Invest in Yourself

Special Message

There is no shortage of motivational speakers in the marketplace today. Most of them rehash old philosophies and methods for change that are no longer relevant in today's society. With the negative lifestyles in which our youth are now growing up in and the rate of teen deaths in society, our youth are faced with what I call the "no need to try" mentality. The youth of today are being raised to just survive and this growing depressed youth culture is faced with unprecedented challenges that test their will to want to secede from society. With that said, it was time for a new, insightful visionary to step forward and motivate our next group of leaders to greatness. *Greatness Now* reaches out and touches the heart and soul of this new generation. The rules in this book truly turn the young readers' dreams into an empowering call to action that goes far beyond their own expectations. Through the reading of this book, the young reader can begin to unlock and activate their "Greatness."

Be Great & **Be Blessed,**
Dr. Charles Carrington

To youth everywhere,
It's time to unlock your GREATNESS.

Acknowlegments

To my parents, Rev. Dr. Charles Carrington and Rev. Dr. Debbie Carrington, thank you for making it possible for me to be able to dream without limits.

To my two beautiful children, Sonny and Monroe, I love you so much. Leaving a legacy for you has become my dream.

To my husband, Matthew, you are my best friend. Thank you for inspiring me and believing in me. Your belief in me gave me no choice but to believe in myself even more.

Introduction

You are special. There is something unique and great about you. You are young, talented, and filled with so much potential to do great things and even change the world!

The choices you make now directly impact your future. In order to achieve your dreams, you must tap into your God-given talents and abilities, which is also known as your *GREATNESS*. You must believe that there are no limits to what you can do and how successful you can become. How you think and feel about yourself matters. The choices you make in your life today matter. The type of friends you hang around matters. How serious you take your education matters. Respect for others matters. Most of the decisions you make now will have an effect on your future success one way or another, so it's time to unlock the greatness that is inside of you so that you can achieve all of your dreams.

Hi, my name is Vameker Banks. I am a Professional School Counselor, Youth Mentor, and Speaker. My goal is to educate and empower youths and young adults by sharing tips and advice for success in school and in life. *Greatness Now: 7 Keys for Teens to Unlock Their Greatness and Achieve Their Dreams* is a fun and easy read designed to help you make the necessary changes in your life so that you are able to become your best self. Enough talk, it's time to unlock your GREATNESS!

Key # 1:

Have A Dream

Realize Your Dreams

If you could do or be anything and money wasn't a factor, what would you want to do or be? What type of life do you want for yourself? This is the time in your life to figure out what you want to do and who you want to become. The sooner you realize what your dreams are, the sooner you can start preparing to make them come true.

Your dreams are the things that make you happy and can ultimately change your life and possibly the lives of others. They are the answers to the *one-day* questions. You know, *one day, I want to…*Take a moment to think about what you want to accomplish, what makes you happy, and what will make your life better. Whatever the answers are to those questions are your dreams. Realizing your dream includes identifying what you are really good at and working hard to become great at it.

Bankable Tip:
If your dreams don't scare you, they're not big enough.

Media Dreams

Social media has a way of making you focus on everyone else but yourself. It is difficult to separate your dreams from what you see on social media. With so many influential people, entertainers, athletes, and other successful people posting about how they live, it makes you think you want to do what they do. That's the power of social media. Don't lose sight of your goals and what you want to be. There are many successful people in the world that live very well. There are doctors, lawyers, businessmen and women, scientists, entrepreneurs, and countless other professionals, living just as well if not better, owning the same things as many of the people you see on social media.

When someone is very good at something, it's natural to develop a desire to do what they do, not really understanding the time and effort it takes to develop the talent or skill. Social media posts, rarely if ever, show the hard work, sacrifice and struggles people make and overcome.

Living your best life is the real goal you should have for yourself. One of the best feelings in the world is to wake up every day and get paid to do what you love. Don't confuse your dreams with what you see on social media. When you are able to separate your dreams from what you see on TV and social media, the success and money will come.

Be careful not to confuse someone else's dream with what you are willing to work for. Pursuing your dreams with dedication, determination and drive, will help you to unlock your greatness.

Bankable Tip:
If you don't work toward your dreams, you will find yourself helping someone else fulfill theirs.

Bystander to Your Dreams

The most important person in a bullying situation is the bystander. The bystander is the person that has the most influence at that moment. Think about it, if someone is being bullied, the bystander can either sit back and do nothing or choose to stand up for that person. The bystander forces others around them to make a decision. A bully only has power when they feel like their behavior is acceptable and will not receive any consequences.

When it comes to your dreams, FEAR is the bully. Fear can bully you to the point that you begin to doubt your ability, and no longer want to pursue your dreams. You begin to question if you even deserve for your dreams to come true. Yes, you are capable of achieving your dreams. Yes, you deserve all the desires of your heart, and yes, fear will creep in from time to time, but you must not allow it stop you from working towards your dreams.

Starting today, no more standing by and allowing fear to bully your dreams. If you want it bad enough, you are going to have to fight for it. Don't worry, if you keep working hard and never give up, my money is on you to win!

Bankable Tip:
Don't stand by and allow fear to bully your dreams.

Fight for Your Dreams

Don't put your dreams off. Remember the title of this book is **Greatness NOW!** Stop thinking you are too young or that you have to wait until later in life to set life goals. Waiting for the right time to pursue your dreams may have you waiting forever.

You don't have to wait until you are older or go away to college to achieve your dreams. There are more and more young people pursuing their dreams and becoming successful at an early age without a college degree. Entrepreneurship has no starting age. That's why it's so important to realize your dreams now. College is not where you decide what you want to be, but rather, a place to go to gain knowledge about what you want to become.

One of the most common feelings you will face while pursuing your dreams is the feeling of wanting to give up. There will also be times when you must go toe-to-toe with your own doubts about your talents and abilities.

Don't let self-doubt trick you into wanting to give up on your dreams. Negative thoughts are a distraction and you must dismiss them immediately.

Anything worth having is worth fighting for. So, put your gloves on and be prepared to fight for your dreams. I guarantee you, it will be worth it. If you stay committed and consistent while pursuing them, they will come true.

Bankable Tip:
Dismiss self-doubt. You have the ability to achieve anything you set your mind to.

Dream Big

When you think about the life you want to live, **dream big**. You deserve it. As the old saying goes, *go big or go home*. When you dream big, you open your mind to endless possibilities. Your dreams should always bring about new dreams. Once you accomplish one, another is born. Don't limit your dreams to make yourself believe they are possible. As cliché as it sounds, whatever your mind can dream of can be achieved. Take a moment to think about the life you want to live. This includes the type of home you want to live in, the kind of car you want to drive, and how much money you want to make. Go ahead, dream really big. Every single thing you just thought about can be yours. You are worthy of having all those things and more!

Now, aside from materialistic things, I want you to think about the contributions you want to make to your family, your community, and the world. The type of person you want to be in life and the legacy you want to leave should be a part of your dream as well. Your dreaming big should also include you making a positive mark in the world. You should also strive to become someone that is kind, thoughtful, and inspires others to want to become a better person too and achieve their dreams.

No matter what your dreams are, keep in mind that just dreaming alone will not make them come true. Hard work, determination, and consistency are imperative. Whose world is this? As my favorite rapper said, the world is yours. Dream big and work hard for the life you want to have. After all, it's your destiny to shine bright, fulfill your purpose, and make all of your dreams come true.

Bankable Tip:
Don't limit your dreams to make yourself believe they are possible.

Dreams into Goals

The best way to achieve your BIG dreams is to break them down. When you think about all the things you want to achieve in life, they can sometimes seem impossible. The best way to combat this overwhelming feeling is to break your dreams down into goals. This means breaking them down, so your mind can process and manage the smaller goals. In turn, you will gain more confidence that you will achieve them too.

It's easier for your brain to process a few small tasks rather than one big task. So, it's best to break your dreams down into goals and break your goals down into action steps.

When working on your dreams, it's important to write them down. Writing things down makes them real. It also helps you to hold yourself accountable of your progress or lack of progress. It is important to check in on your goals often to make sure you are doing what you need to do to make them come true. Don't forget to reward yourself along the way, it's great motivation!

Take a look at the activity on the next page. Think of a dream that you have for your life. Next, think about one goal that you will need to accomplish to put you one step closer towards achieving your dream. Finally, write down what steps you must take to execute your goals.

Bankable Tip:
Turn your dreams into goals and check them off one by one.

How to Turn Your Dreams into Goals:

o What is your dream?

o What is the one thing you must do in order
   to achieve your dream?

o The steps I must take to achieve this goal:

   Action Step 1:

   Action Step 2:

   Action Step 3:

   Action Step 4:

   Action Step 5:

Things to Think About

o Why is having a dream important?

o Think about a time when you were so impressed with how well someone did something that you thought you wanted to do it too, then changed your mind.

o Why is it important to fight for your dreams?

o Why is it important to write down your dreams?

o How does being a bystander to your dream hurt your chances of making your dreams come true?

Greatness Now

Key # 2:

Think Great

Thoughts

Motivated by Your Past

You can't move forward if you are stuck in your past. Sometimes, your past has a way of taking over your thoughts. Don't allow your past to dictate how you think and feel about yourself. Whether it's low grades, poor choices, or fake friends, learn from your past and let it motivate you to work that much harder to achieve your dreams. There are things about your past that you cannot change, so the best thing to do is to make peace with your past and move on. NO COMPLAINING!

Complaining comes from negative thinking and unresolved feelings. It does nothing to help you achieve your dreams. It can create a sense of self-pity and will indeed keep you from living the life you deserve. Allow your past to be your motivation to want to do better and be a better person.

There are so many people that cannot let go of their past mistakes and it stops them from growing into the person they are meant to become. When you are always thinking about your past, seeking sympathy, or hoping for a handout, you are stifling your greatness. So, let go of last year's failures and mistakes and stop thinking the world owes you something. Your past does not determine your future. Use your past as a reminder of what you don't want so you will work harder for what you do want.

If you are focusing on your past more than your future, you make it difficult to give your dreams and goals the attention they deserve. Your past has a major effect on what you think of yourself but does not determine how successful you will be in the future. So, leave your past in the past so you can unlock your greatness for a better future.

Bankable Tip:
Don't allow your past to dictate how you think and feel about yourself.

Do the Right Thing

Doing the right thing requires you to think more positively. When you think better, you do better, because your thoughts influence how you act. When you think negatively, you are more likely to act in a negative way. When you think positively, you tend to act in a more positive way. When you think positively, you also become more aware of all the positive things in your life and begin to appreciate them more. Hold yourself to a higher standard, and your behavior, attitude, and work ethic will all change because of your positive thoughts about yourself. You develop a desire for positivity in your life, and in turn, you do more positive things for others.

Doing the right thing is not hard. In this world of *what's in it for me* thinking, we have lost sight of the importance of doing the right thing just because it's the right thing. Sometimes, you may feel pressure to do something because it's popular rather than right.

Doing the right thing may seem challenging, but it will never make you question your beliefs or values. You are in charge of you. You should always strive to do the right thing. You are old enough now, where the expectation to do the right thing is upon you. No longer does the excuse of not knowing or being too young apply. Aside from the expectation from your parents, you should have greater expectations of yourself and that should include you being able to make tough decisions and doing what is right.

Bankable Tip:
Discipline is doing the right thing when it's hard and when no one is watching.

Believe in Yourself

If you don't believe in yourself, how can you expect anyone else to believe in you? I have worked with so many teens that just don't believe they are capable of being successful in life. They are not aware of their talents and abilities, so they just don't believe in themselves. In order to unlock your greatness, you must change your thinking and start believing in yourself.

The more you tell yourself how great you are, the more you will believe it and even start acting like it. Believing in yourself and building up your self-confidence doesn't happen overnight or by reading a good book. You must talk to yourself in a positive way every day. You have to know that you are worthy of success, happiness, and all the desires of your heart, no matter your past or even current situation. You must surround yourself with positive people that have dreams too. Sometimes, it takes being around others who are positive for you to become more positive. Sometimes, it takes someone else believing in you so much that you start believing in yourself.

One of the most harmful things you can do to yourself is not believing in yourself. You are capable of achieving anything you put your mind to. You are someone that is going to make a difference in this world. The more you think positively about yourself, the more you will believe in yourself. The more you believe in yourself, the more you will activate your greatness and begin to achieve your dreams.

Bankable Tip:
The most harmful thing you can do to yourself is not believing in yourself.

Affirm Your Greatness

When you affirm who you are, you remind yourself of just how great you are. You focus on all the positive things that you have to offer. You also encourage and empower yourself to be great and achieve great things in your life. Affirming yourself, helps to block out what others say and think about you so, when you are faced with a negative comment or situation, you come out unbothered. It doesn't matter what anyone else says about you because the only opinion that matters is your own. Get in the habit of affirming yourself each and every day. You can say positive things about yourself to yourself. You can write them down in a journal and refer to them often. You can listen to or watch motivational videos. Now that you know how to affirm your greatness, it's time to reintroduce yourself to the world!

Bankable Tip:
Don't allow people to tell you who you are. You tell people who you are.

Greatness Affirmation

I am Great. I was created by Greatness to be Great. Greatness is in my DNA; therefore, I am destined for Greatness. It doesn't matter what anyone else says because I know I am Great. I say I am Great. Anything I put my mind to, I will achieve, and it will be Great. For I know just by saying I am Great is not enough. I must BELIEVE I am Great and put in Great work to unlock the Greatness that is inside of me. I must dream Great dreams, think Great thoughts, and do Great deeds. I will show the world how Great I am so that no one will doubt my Greatness, Not Even Me!

Things to Think About

o On a scale of 1-10, how much do you believe in yourself?

o What are three things that you love about yourself? Why?

o When was the last time you made the decision to do the right thing even though it felt difficult to do? Why was it difficult?

o Why is it important to affirm who you are everyday?

o Think about something bad that happened in your past that you will use as your motivation going forward.

Greatness Now

Key # 3:

Elevate Your Effort

Evaluate and Elevate

Have you ever felt like you did your best but your best just wasn't good enough? How much effort you put into your goals will determine how successful you will be at achieving them. Now is the time to evaluate and elevate your effort.

Take a moment to evaluate the amount of effort you have been giving to your education, your dreams, and your friendships. Are you really giving your best effort? That test that you didn't do well on, could you have studied longer and sooner? That friendship that is strained, did you really try to understand how your friend felt about the disagreement? When you evaluate the effort, you give to all the things you care about and want to change or improve in your life, I bet you could give a little more effort.

So now that you have evaluated your effort, it's time to elevate it. Your best effort means giving a little more than you thought you had left to give. It means not giving up, ever. There may be some nights where you are up late working on a project or studying. Greatness requires you to put in longer hours sometimes to get things done.

When you elevate your effort, you work extra hard to achieve your goals. You are super focused. You dismiss distractions, eliminate excuses, and focus on your future. All of these things are necessary because excellence should be the expectation for yourself and from yourself.

Bankable Tip:
Do your best and forget the rest.

Excellence is the New Expectation

If you expect nothing but great things to happen in your life, guess what? More great things will begin to happen in your life. This does not mean that bad things won't happen, but it does help you to focus on all the positive things and be more appreciative of them. Your perception becomes your reality. When you focus on all the positive things in your life, you give more effort to them. What you think about most gets most of your time and attention.

In order to have success in school and in life, you must dare to dream and have the audacity to hope. If you don't dream great dreams, think great thoughts, or speak great things into your life, how can you expect to attract greatness into your life?

Expectations are standards of what is and is not acceptable to you. Since excellence is the expectation, average and mediocre effort should not be acceptable to you. You should always give your best effort in everything you do.

Think about your favorite entertainer or athlete. They are the best at what they do because they never give mediocre effort. The expectation from themselves is always excellence. Excellence should be your personal expectation at all times. You should give your best in everything you do. When you do your best and put in maximum effort, you will see excellence emerge. Few people are willing to work hard. Most want things to be easy. Be willing to work for what you want and make sure to always give your best effort. In whatever you do, excellence should always be your expectation of yourself.

Bankable Tip:
Make excellence your personal expectation.

Good vs. Great

Who wants to be good when you can be GREAT?! The goal is to be so great that you leave people in awe! In order to be considered great, you have to go above and beyond what you are used to doing. You must move from good to great! What separates the good from the great? The good study, but the great study after they are tired of studying. The good put in effort, practice, and are competitive. But the great put in effort on top of effort. They practice after practice is over, and they are competitive with themselves. They are always striving to be better than they were yesterday. They use their dreams as their motivation and never give up on themselves. They have a standard of excellence, so average is unacceptable.

You are a young person full of greatness and the great are never okay with average. You should never be okay with average grades, average friends, or average effort.

Figure out what you really want to devote your energy to and then take the time to become great at it. You must give more effort than you have been giving if you want to be great. Talent does play a factor, but hard work, a great attitude, and effort separates you from the rest. Don't talk about wanting to be the best. Do what it takes to become *your* best. Nothing you do from now on should be average, nor should you be afraid to be awesome. The good strive for average, the great strive to be awesome. So, I ask you again, who wants to be good when you can be GREAT?!

Bankable Tip:
It's time to move from average to awesome.

Things to Think About

o What are your expectations for your life?

o On a scale of 1-10, how much effort are you giving to your dreams?

o How have your expectations of yourself affected your effort? (high expectations, high effort; low expectations, low effort.)

o What are the advantages of having high expectations for yourself?

o What do you need to do to move from good to great?

Key # 4:

Invest In Yourself

Care About Your Education

T he best thing you can do for yourself is to make a serious investment in your education. It's time you care more about your education. When you care about your education, it means you care about your future. Caring, gives your teachers and parents' permission to care more. They will invest their time, energy, and even money to see to it that your dreams come true. So, never let anyone care more about something concerning you than you. The moment someone else cares more about your goals, dreams, and education, you lose control over your happiness and success. You must act and speak in a way that lets people know you care about your education and that you are in control.

Your parents and teachers are there to support you in achieving your dreams. If you don't care about your success in school, then they can't support you like you want them to.

Being able to achieve your dreams is determined by how much you care. Make your education a priority. Take responsibility for what you need to do to be successful in school. Care, and care more than anyone else.

Bankable Tip:
When you care, you give others permission to care too.

Take Responsibility

There are very few things that you are responsible for at this moment in your life. Your education happens to be one of them. Your education is not something that you want to put into someone else's hands. It should be more important to you than anything else, and it's time you make it a priority.

Teachers are responsible for teaching. This may be hard to do with so many distractions in the classroom today. Just make sure you are not one of them. You must be an example to your peers. You should be asking questions in class and showing your teacher and peers that your education is important to you. Stop worrying about what your friends and classmates will say. Chances are they have the same question as you and will follow your lead of making education a priority.

Not only does taking responsibility for your education show leadership and great character, it will also increase your success in school. When you take responsibility for your education, you will begin to see your grades improve, your relationships with your teachers improve, and your excitement for your education increase. Your education is not your parents' responsibility nor is it your teachers' responsibility. Your education is your responsibility. When you take responsibility for your education, you create more opportunities for yourself, and you are one step closer to achieving your dreams.

Bankable Tip:
Your success in school depends on you taking responsibility for your own education.

Ask for Help

Asking for help shows strength. Sometimes, you get caught up in what you think people will think about you when you ask for help. Why is it so difficult to ask for help? Well, because some people think it's a sign of weakness and that's just not true. Strong, smart, and successful people are always asking for help.

I would often ask students that were sent to my office if they didn't understand something in class, why they didn't ask the teacher for help. The answer was pretty unanimous. Over the years, students have told me the number one reason for not asking questions in class is because they don't want to look stupid.

Don't ever be scared to ask questions in class. You don't have to put pressure on yourself to understand something the first, second, or even the third time it is explained. It takes time to learn new things. Almost everything is hard at first. Get in the habit of reading things two or three times. It increases your understanding of the information and can lead to you asking fewer questions in class. After reading and re-reading, if you still don't understand, then just ask for help.

One of the differences between students who do well in school and those who could do better is that students who do well have help. Whether they have help at school or at home, they are receiving help from someone, somewhere. Don't assume they were just born smart. Asking for help shows your interest and commitment to your education.

Why Ask Why?

When you were younger, one of your favorite questions to ask was WHY? You probably asked why about everything to the point that you got on your parents' nerves. Somewhere along the way, you lost your WHY. WHY is one of the most important questions you could ever ask. WHY, you ask? Well, it leads to knowledge and knowledge leads to better opportunities.

Start asking WHY when people share information with you. Make it a habit to do your own research, especially when it comes to information on the internet. Everything you see and hear is not real or true and should be investigated thoroughly.

In order to unlock your greatness, asking questions and asking for help must become a part of what you do often. When you ask questions, you get answers. When you get answers, you are that much closer to achieving your dreams!

Bankable Tip:
When you ask questions, you get answers. Start asking more questions.

Education Empowers

Education leads to empowerment; and empowerment leads to making a difference in the world. Education is needed to take advantage of so many future opportunities waiting for you. When you take control of your education, you create opportunities that you didn't even know existed. You need opportunities to achieve your dreams. That is why education is so important. Education is not just about the information you learn in school. Education is a life-long process that includes using what you learn in school to help you create the life you dream of. The right education will empower you to help others live a better life too.

Education is power, and that power empowers you. Education is the best form of empowerment because once you know something, you know it forever! You can use what you know to make a difference in the world.

Bankable Tip:
Education is needed to fuel your dreams.

Things to Think About

o Name the top three things you care about the most and why.

o Why is it important to care about your education more than anyone else?

o Is it hard for you to ask for help in class? Why?

o At what age or grade does education become a child's responsibility? Why?

o Do your parents and teachers believe you really care about your education? How do you know?

Greatness Now

Key # 5:

Partner with Your Parents

It's A Partnership

A partnership means working together to achieve a goal. Your parents are the first partners you have in life. Their goal is to help you live a successful and happy life. No matter what you think about your parents or how they make you feel, you need them. Don't assume you can become successful all on your own. In order to reach your full potential, you must build good relationships in life, and the absolute most important relationship that you should have right now is the one with your parents. Your parents have and will continue to invest their time, money, and efforts to help you unlock your greatness and achieve your dreams. Don't shut them out, even when they get on your nerves. They are the only people that will invest in you and your dream and not expect anything in return.

If your goals in life require you to attend

college, chances are your parents are going to do whatever they can, including getting a second or third job, cutting back on spending, or even taking out a loan just to help you go to college and achieve your dream. Given all the sacrifices your parents are willing to make to help you achieve your dreams, it's time for you to start doing your part when it comes to your education and life choices. You should strive to do better and make better choices.

Parents are not friends. They are your parents. Their job is to guide you to greatness and hold you accountable to the expectations set for you. They give you what you need so that one day, you can get the things you want. It's time to start viewing your parents as your success partners. Achieving your dreams is a lot easier when you have a partner that has your back no matter what.

Bankable Tip:
Your relationship with your parents should also be a partnership.

Parents Just Don't Understand

Contrary to what you think, your parents have a lot of life experience. They have been through many of the same things you have and will go through in life. So why are they so annoying at times? It's simple. There is a clash of the generations! Every generation goes through this, so consider it a rite of passage. Your parents are old-school and you are new-school. One day, you will be considered old-school and the generation after you will be new-school. Your parents were brought up in a different time where they experienced the same things as you but were able to handle them in a different way, because of the times. But just because times change, don't mean methods do. Many of the old-school methods still apply today. They also just want to shield you from anything they think may hurt you or hold you back.

You, on the other hand, want to experience things for yourself even if there may be a tough lesson to learn. After all, you just want to live your life, right? Well, listening to your parents will help you live a long life. The scripture says, *"Children, obey your parents so that your days may be long."* It's true! Think back to when you were younger, and your mom or dad told you not to do something and you did it anyway, what happened? You ended up hurting yourself. So, don't argue with your parents about everything you don't agree with or think is unfair. You must pick and choose your battles. If you argue and have an attitude about everything, nothing will stand out as being really important to you. Therefore, it won't become important to them.

Arguing with your parents all the time puts a strain on your relationship too. You cannot develop a good relationship when all you do is argue and have an attitude. Even though you get frustrated with your parents, don't shut them out.

Despite their approach, their tone, their rules, and oftentimes, their seemingly unfair reasons for why you cannot do something or go somewhere, your parents only want the best for you. They don't want you to go through the same things they did growing up or even worse. There is a lot that you don't know. You think you know, but you have no idea. Yes, there are some things you do know but they have good reason to be unfair (*in your eyes*). There is going to be a time in your life when you look back and thank your parents for being *unfair*. Trust me.

They always have the absolute best intentions and are coming from a loving place with all that they do for you. Your parents were young too and their parents didn't understand them either. I bet they didn't think they would be parenting the way they are. Who knows, one day, you will look back and your children will be talking about how unfair you are; and how much you just don't understand. But in the meantime, cut your parents some slack.

Bankable Tip:
Your goal should not just be to be understood by your parents, it should be to have an understanding with them.

Honor Your Parents

What does it mean to honor your parents? It means to be the person they have raised you to be. It means you are making good decisions and staying true to your core values. It means you do things to make your parents proud.

When you leave the house, you are a reflection of your parents and honoring them should be an expectation you have for yourself. What they have taught you should come to mind whenever you are hanging out with friends or in an uncomfortable situation.

Respect goes hand in hand when it comes to honoring your parents. Respecting your parents means to talk to them in a loving tone. Respect is not talking back, staying out of trouble, doing your best in school, and making good choices. Just in case you want to know how else to honor and respect your parents, take a look at the 10 Commandments on the next page and decide which one(s) you need to work on to honor your parents more.

Bankable Tip:
Don't just defend your mother's honor when someone talks about her, honor her by making good choices and knowing when to walk away.

The 10 Commandments

1. I shall say, "I love you" often.

2. I shall do what needs to be done without being asked.

3. I shall not talk back.

4. I shall stop thinking I know more than my parents.

5. I shall work hard in school.

6. I shall appreciate my parents more.

7. I shall hold my tongue when my parents say something that upsets me.

8. I shall make good decisions when my parents are not around.

9. I shall not argue with my parents.

10. I shall make an effort to make my parents proud.

Things to Think About

o What do you want your parents to do more of to help you achieve your goals?

o How do you plan to honor your parents outside of the home?

o When was the last time you talked to your parents about something that was really important to you? Did it turn into an argument? Why? What would you do differently?

o What are three things you are thankful for about your parents?

o Which commandment(s) do you need to work on the most and why?

Greatness Now

Key # 6:

Have Great Friends

Fake vs. Great

Don't be so quick to use the word *friend*. Be selective with whom you will allow around the greatness that is in you!

The number of friends you have doesn't make you any better than anyone else. Popularity is not what you should strive for, but rather, being a good person and a great friend to others. The time will come if it has not already, to figure out who are your real friends and who are not.

So, what is the difference between fake friends and great friends? Fake friends are always making poor choices and getting into trouble. They pressure you into doing things that make you uncomfortable and go against the values that you have been taught at home.

They smile in your face and talk behind your

back. They get mad about everything and not willing to work out disagreements.

Anytime you question your friendships, you might need to start looking for some new friends. Great friends, however, do things to help you become a better person. You don't have to question their intentions. They value your friendship and treat you with respect. Great friends want to work with you and value who you are as a person. Do you have friends that value you as a person? If not, you should reevaluate your friendships. Not only should you surround yourself with great people, but you also have to be a great friend to others. Be the type of friend you want to have.

In order to unlock your greatness, you must surround yourself with people that are great and want you to be great too. It's time for you to get rid of your fake friends and start hanging out with some great friends.

Bankable Tip:
Get rid of those fake friends and get you some great friends!

10 Ways to Spot a Fake Friend:

1. Only talk about themselves.

2. Try to get you to do something that is wrong.

3. Make bad choices often.

4. Jealous of you or what you have achieved.

5. Competitive with you on everything.

6. Use you to get closer to others.

7. Don't make an effort to work out a petty disagreement.

8. Leaves you to handle a bad situation they were a part of.

9. Don't keep their promises.

10. Does something for you and expect something in return.

Forever Friendships

Everyone that you hang out with now are not meant to be your friends forever. People come into your life for a reason, a season, and a few stay for a lifetime. Many of the people you consider your friends now may not be your friends later in life. It's not that they are bad people, it's just that people grow apart.

Think about it, are the friends you had in elementary school your friends now? If not, it's okay because, your interests change as you grow older. Your friends should be a positive influence in your life. As you grow and change, so should your friends. Maybe you were quiet before and now you're more outspoken. Maybe you weren't really into school and now that you're older, you are taking it more seriously. Change is good. Don't associate personal growth as bad or *fake*. Personal growth means becoming better. Do you want to stay the same or become better? Do you want your friends to stay the same or become better?

Your friendships play a key role in you becoming better. Great people have great people around them to help bring out the greatness within them. Think about the people you call your friends now, are they really the kind of people you want to have in your life forever?

Bankable Tip:
Everybody is not meant to be your friend forever.

The Right Influence

At this stage of your life, your friendships are very important. They play a huge role in how you see yourself and how you see the world. Your friends influence how you think, feel, and behave.

Depending on your friends, you may feel like school sucks because it sucks to them. Depending on your friends, you may choose not to like someone because they don't like them. Depending on your friends, you may act a certain way just to gain attention, even though it's totally out of character for you to act that way.

Friendships matter. Who you are around most of the time is a direct reflection of your judgement and the type of person you may become. You can be the most caring person in the world but because you hang around someone who is petty, you begin to act petty. In order to be your best self, you must surround yourself around the right influences.

Think about who you hang around in school and outside of school. Ask yourself if they are great friends or fake friends. If they are fake, then you need to get rid of them and find friends that are of good influence. Make a promise to yourself today that you will start hanging around people that bring out the best in you.

Bankable Tip:
Who you are around most of the time is a direct reflection on the type of person you are and will become.

Things to Think About

o Do you consider yourself a great friend? Why?

o What are the most important qualities a friend should have? Why?

o Do your parents know the people you consider your friends? Why or Why not?

o Why do people think they have to have a lot of friends?

o What are some benefits of having great friends in your life?

Key # 7:

Manage Your Life

Take Charge

Sometimes, your life can feel like a mess. It's up to you to take charge and manage your life. Who is in charge of you? You. Who is in charge of your emotions? You. Who is in charge of how you use your time? You. You must hold yourself to higher standards. What does this mean? This means you cannot get upset every time something bothers you. Don't blame other people for your actions. Respond, don't react in stressful situations. Value your time. Doing all these things will help you to take charge of your life.

Bankable Tip:
When you manage your life better, life gets better.

Respond, Don't React

People are going to do and say things that get on your nerves all the time. There are also going to be times when you get stressed out. In order to unlock your greatness, you have to learn how to manage your emotions. You must learn the art of responding, rather than reacting. When you respond, you take some time to think about what to say or do in the situation. When you react, you do things without thinking about the consequences of your actions.

Everything should not bother you to the point that you feel the need to go off, cuss, or fight someone. Pick and choose what you will allow to upset you. That's called self-control. Chances are most things that upset you are not even worth you being mad over. Nothing should upset you to the point that you are in a constant state of unhappiness and stress. If you are, I STRONGLY encourage you to reach out and talk to someone about your feelings. Being strong doesn't mean to hold your feelings in. Being strong is being aware of things that bother you, responding, not reacting to them, and asking for help when you need it.

You are allowed to feel the way you feel. If you're happy, be happy. If you're upset, be upset. If you're angry, be angry. Anger is an emotion. Being angry and doing things out of anger are two totally different things. You can be angry at your teacher for calling you out in front of all your peers in class, but you should not curse at your teacher. You can be upset with your friend about something they said, but it shouldn't get physical nor should you let things that people say or do stress you out.

You ever feel like there is so much to do and so little time? Yep, that's stress. Stress is a part of life; and unfortunately, will come up from time to time throughout your life. Learning how to manage your stress now is going to help you know how to manage your stress in the future.

The best way to manage your stress is to take a break and do more of what you love. Take a look at 10 ways to manage your stress. Which one(s) do you need to incorporate into your life to decrease your stress? In order to unlock your greatness, managing your stress is very imperative.

Bankable Tip:
To avoid stress, get some rest, do your best, and avoid mess.

10 Ways to Manage Your Stress

1. Don't wait until the last minute.

2. Get more sleep.

3. Break down large tasks.

4. Participate in clubs and activities.

5. Exercise often.

6. Volunteer in your community.

7. Do things that make you happy.

8. Don't hang around negative people.

9. Ask for help when you need it.

10. Talk to someone about what is stressing you out.

Value Your Time

Your time is valuable. Don't give it all away to others, keep some for yourself. Time management is a skill that if not learned early in life, can delay or even stop you from accomplishing your goals. You must take a time-out from time to time in order to unlock your greatness. You must decide what is important to you and then give them the attention they deserve. Family, education, and your future are all the things that should be on your list. Think about some of the things that you do now that takes time away from you devoting time to the things that are important. Some common time-takers that teens face are; hanging out with friends **too much**, watching **too much** TV, or spending **too much** time doing nothing. You can and should still spend time doing the things that you enjoy; just understand that spending time doing nothing or too much of anything is not a good use of your time.

You should be doing something productive at all times. If you are not studying for school, you could be at practice. If you are not at practice, you could be volunteering. If you are not volunteering, you could be doing your chores. If you are not doing your chores, you could be at church. If you are not at church, you could be helping your younger brother or sister. If you don't have any younger brothers or sisters, you could be helping someone in the community. If you are not helping someone in the community, you could be working on an idea that you came up with and figuring out how to make money from it. See, there is no short list of *valuable* things you could be doing with your time. When you are busy with activities, you don't have time to be bored. Being involved in a club, sport, or activity leaves little time to be bored or get into trouble. It also helps mold you into the wonderful person you are destined to be.

Knowing how to manage time is a difficult thing, not just for teens but adults too. Time is definitely something that must be managed and monitored often. If you don't know how to manage your time now, it's going to be very difficult for you to manage your time later in life. Take a look at the 10 ways to manage your time on the next page. Which one(s) stand out to you? Which one do you plan to implement in order to manage your time better going forward? Remember, whatever you do with your time now has a huge impact on you being able to achieve your dreams. When you value your time, others will.

Bankable Tip:
Time will tell if you managed your time well. Focusing on what doesn't matter takes time away from what does.

10 Ways to Value Your Time

1. Plan ahead.

2. Make a to-do list.

3. Use an agenda/planner.

4. Learn to say No.

5. Have a morning and nightly routine.

6. Start on tasks as soon as you get them.

7. Organize and reorganize as needed.

8. Limit your social media usage.

9. Prioritize important things first.

10. Take breaks often.

Social Media

One of the biggest distractions today is social media. Your social media accounts have become your online resume. Whatever you post, like, or share is tracked. Keep in mind that it can and may be used against you in the future. On average, teens spend more time on social media than they do in school each day. Take a moment to answer these two questions. How much time are you spending on social media each day? What is the latest you've stayed up because you were on your phone? You must not only manage how much time you spend on social media, but you must also manage what you are watching and posting when you're on it. There is so much negativity on social media, so it's easy to get caught up in it. But remember, you are a great person and must conduct yourself accordingly. Don't post or get involved in mess. Yes, you can have an opinion about things, but you don't have to comment on everything you see and read. If so, that can be viewed as cyberbullying, and you definitely don't want to get caught up in that!

Cyberbullying is a very serious issue that teens face today. It involves the trolling of others on social media and posting negative things. Because you are on a mission to unlock your greatness, you must hold yourself to a higher standard, especially on social media. If you don't, your social media behavior will block you from future opportunities. Businesses and colleges track what you post on your social media accounts. So, be smart about what you post.

Social media can be addictive. It's hard to pull yourself away from it. Try setting time aside each day for being on social media, then log off. The reward of managing how much time you spend on social media and what you view and post on it is priceless. If you can learn to manage your media intake, you can really focus on making your dreams come true.

Bankable Tip:
Real strength is measured by what you can do without.

Messy Conversations

Messy thoughts lead to messy conversations; and messy conversations lead to messy behaviors and choices. Sometimes, people say things out of jealousy or to make themselves feel good. People are going to talk about you no matter what you do, good or bad. Don't be *that* person. Don't talk about others to feel better, you won't. Any time you find yourself talking about someone, make sure you are speaking from a positive and honest place; and not doing it to be messy and hurtful. When I was a school counselor, I had girls come to my office daily about *she said, she said* drama. It always started with someone saying what someone else said. I know, messy, right? The best way to avoid this kind of drama is to manage your conversations. Talking about someone doesn't make you cool or tough.

Having great conversations are about choosing to have positive conversations that encourage and empower, not belittle and tear someone down. Don't put yourself in a situation where you are engaging in messy conversations. Most mess between friends starts with negative comments and conversations. Talking about people is a waste of time and energy, and it adds no value to your life.

Learn to walk away from messy conversations that encourage you to make negative comments. When you choose not to engage in negative conversations, you don't have to worry about someone saying you said something you didn't say.

Remember, in order to become your greatest self, you must have positive conversations that focus on positive things. When you give off positive vibes, you get positive vibes back. Great conversations help you to attract positive things into your life. You never know who knows who and can create an opportunity for you to share your gifts and talents. When you let go of messy conversations, and engage in positive talk with yourself and others, you are able to unlock your greatness and achieve all your dreams.

Bankable Tip:
Learn to walk away from conversations that influence you to make negative comments about others.

Things to Think About

o What areas of your life do you feel are a bit messy? Why?

o Think of a time that you reacted and should have responded in a negative or stressful situation. What would you do differently?

o How do you feel when you don't manage your time well? What are you going to do about it?

o Why is it important to manage your media intake?

o Why is it important to stay out of messy conversations?

A Final Word

I hope by reading this book, you were able to reflect on all of the wonderful things about you; and recognize what changes you need to make to become an even better you. My goal was to give you things to think about and spark a desire for you to unlock your greatness by applying what I have shared. If you implement the seven keys outlined in this book into your life, then there is no limit to how great you will become. Now that you know what you need to do to unlock your greatness, I challenge you to go out into the world and share your **GREATNESS NOW!**

About the Author

Vameker Banks is a Character Education Counselor, Author and Speaker. She holds a bachelor's degree in Psychology and a master's degree in Urban School Counseling. She served in the Gwinnett County Public School System for six years as a school counselor, peer leader teacher, and parent involvement coordinator.

Her mission is to educate, encourage and empower youths and young adults to be the best version of themselves by sharing tips and expert advice to help them master the life skills needed to live a confident and happy life.

25744725R00057

Made in the USA
Columbia, SC
06 September 2018